D1459611

Origami, simply put, is the art of folding paper.
But origami is so much more than just folded paper. It is geometry,
poetry, sculpture, and design. In origami, a relatively small
number of standard folds are used to create an almost infinite
number of forms, ranging from the very simple to extremely
complex. These forms can be literal and representational, or
abstract and evocative.

The projects in the *Origami Craft Pad: Creatures & Critters* are all
familiar. Some are animals, and some are insects. Some are old,
and some are new. All of them can be made with any square sheet
of relatively thin paper—this craft pad contains 75 sheets of
beautifully patterned paper for you to make anything you like.
Some projects will require a pair of scissors. Outlined on the first
pages of these instructions are some basic folds and bases you will
use time and again for your projects. If you are completely new to
origami, practicing these folds will provide a good warm-up for
making the cute and friendly critters included here. And even if
you aren't new to origami, it is always a good idea to do a practice
run using plain paper.

Finished origami projects may be seen as little art pieces unto
themselves, but they can also be combined to create a menagerie.
They may be used as adornments on gifts, or fashioned into
mobiles. They can be attached to magnets to decorate your
refrigerator, or to pinbacks and worn as fashion accessories.
The possibilities are endless. All you need is your imagination,
and a pretty square of paper. **Happy folding!**

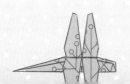

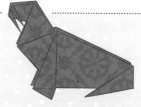

FOLD ARROW
Fold in the direction of the arrow.

FOLD BEHIND ARROW
Fold behind in the direction of the arrow.

FOLD AND UNFOLD ARROW
Fold and unfold in the direction of the arrow.

TURN OVER SYMBOL
Turn the project or paper over.

ROTATE SYMBOL
Rotate the project or paper.

PULL OUT ARROW
Pull out as indicated.

CUT SYMBOL
Carefully cut paper as indicated with scissors or an X-Acto knife.

arrows and symbols

These standard symbols will appear in the instructions for the various projects contained in this book and will help you to understand the diagrams.

basic folds

Origami employs a number of basic folds, from very simple to somewhat tricky. Practice these basic folds on less fancy paper before attempting to make a project. When practicing, experiment with different angles and proportions and see how doing so affects the end result.

VALLEY FOLD
Valley fold line.

Fold so the valley fold line is on the inside of the fold.

completed valley fold

MOUNTAIN FOLD
Mountain fold line

Fold so the mountain fold line is on the outside.

completed mountain fold

INSIDE REVERSE FOLD
STEP 1: Fold and unfold to create a crease.

STEP 2: Gently pull sides apart while pushing center flap down between them (fold flap between them).

completed inside reverse fold

OUTSIDE REVERSE FOLD
STEP 1: Fold and unfold to create a crease.

STEP 2: Gently pull sides apart and down while pushing center in between them (fold flap to the outside).

completed outside reverse fold

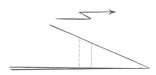

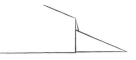

PLEAT FOLD
A pleat fold combines valley and mountain folds to create a fold that is somewhat like a stair step.

STEP 1: Make valley and mountain folds where indicated.

STEP 2: Fold in along the mountain line and back out along the valley line to complete the pleat fold.

basic folds

bases

Countless origami projects can be made from a handful of standard bases. It is a good idea to practice with less fancy paper first. Unlike the basic folds, it is essential that you follow the instructions precisely every time.

PRELIMINARY BASE

STEP 1: Make creases by folding and unfolding from corner to corner.

STEP 2: Turn over.

STEP 3: Make creases by folding and unfolding from side to side.

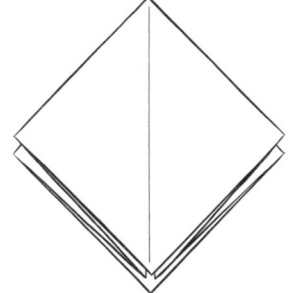

STEP 4: Bring the outer corners up, then down toward the bottom corner, then bring the top corner down.

completed preliminary base

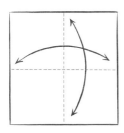

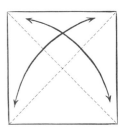

TRIANGLE BASE

STEP 1: Make creases by folding and unfolding from side to side.

STEP 2: Turn over.

STEP 3: Make creases by folding and unfolding from corner to corner.

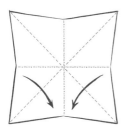

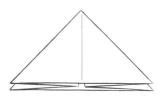

STEP 4: Bring the creases at the center of the sides down to the crease at the center of the bottom and collapse the shape.

completed triangle base

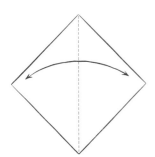

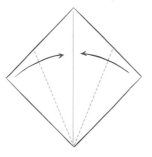

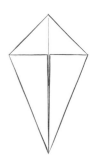

KITE BASE

STEP 1: Fold and unfold.

STEP 2: Fold outer corners toward center.

completed kite base

bases

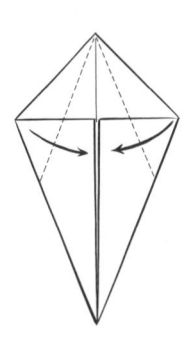

DIAMOND BASE

STEP 1: Begin with a completed kite base.

STEP 2: Fold the outer corners in toward center.

completed diamond base

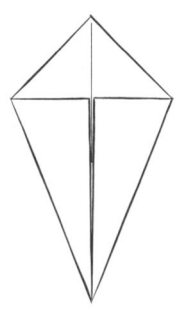

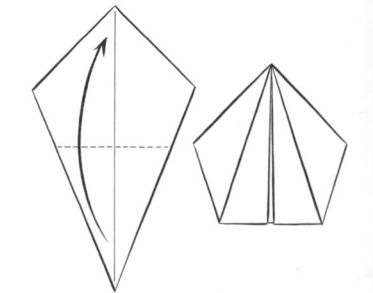

FISH BASE

STEP 1: Begin with a completed kite base.

STEP 2: Turn over.

STEP 3: Fold up.

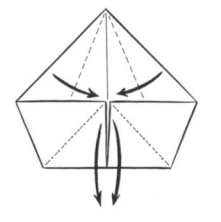
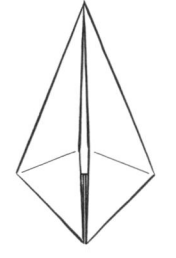

STEP 4: Turn over.

STEP 5: Fold outer corners in while folding inner corners down.

completed fish base.

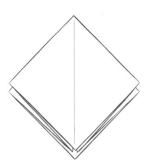

BIRD BASE

STEP 1: Begin with a completed preliminary base.

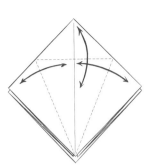

STEP 2: Make creases by folding and unfolding the outer and upper corners.

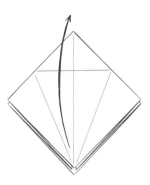

STEP 3: Fold only the uppermost layer of the bottom corner up.

STEP 4: The outer corners of the upper layer will flatten

and move in toward the center.

STEP 5: Turn over.

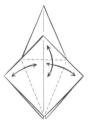

STEP 6: Fold and unfold the outer and upper corners as on the previous side.

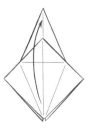

STEP 7: Fold the upper layer of the bottom corner up as on the previous side.

completed bird base

bases

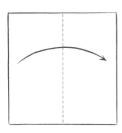

STEP 1: Fold paper in half horizontally.

STEP 2: Fold and unfold vertically to make a crease.

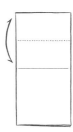

STEP 3: Fold and unfold the top half behind to create a mountain crease.

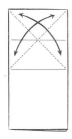

STEP 4: Fold and unfold top square diagonally.

STEP 5: Fold the sides in to create a triangle.

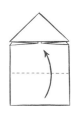

STEP 6: Fold up.

STEP 7: Fold sides in.

STEP 8: Fold bottom up.

STEP 9: Fold corners down.

frog

This frog, once completed, can actually be made to jump! Have a friend make one, too, and see which frog can jump the highest and farthest.

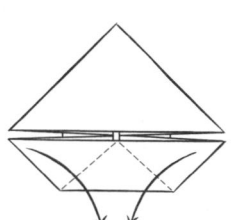

STEP 10: Pull out.

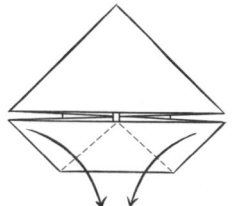

STEP 11: Fold points down.

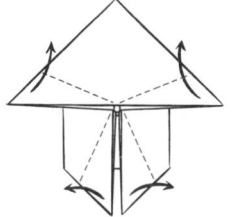

STEP 12: Fold top points up, and bottom points out.

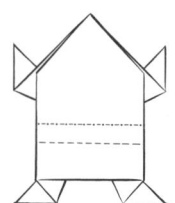

STEP 13: Turn over.

STEP 14: Make a pleat fold.

completed frog

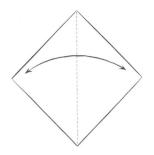

STEP 1: Fold and unfold.

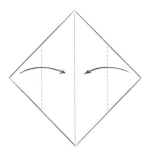

STEP 2: Fold side corners into the center.

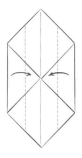

STEP 3: Fold sides in.

STEP 4: Fold sides in again.

STEP 5: Rotate.

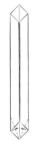

STEP 6: Fold bottom corners into the center.

STEP 7: Fold in half vertically.

STEP 8: Fold up to make an outside reverse fold for the neck.

STEP 9: Make another outside reverse fold for the head.

snake

Ssss. . . . This skinny, slithery snake is a great project for beginners.

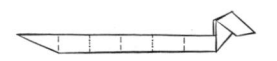 

STEP 10: Make alternating valley and mountain folds to make the snake slither.

completed snake

STEP 1: Begin with completed triangle base turned upside-down.

STEP 2: Fold top corners down.

STEP 3: Turn over.

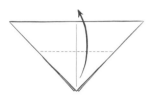

STEP 4: Fold up.

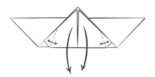

STEP 5: Fold and unfold side corners to create creases, then pull top two points down.

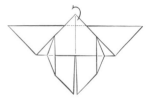

STEP 6: Fold top point over to the back.

STEP 7: Fold in half vertically.

STEP 8: Fold wings forward.

completed butterfly.

butterfly

This colorful winged creature is one of nature's greatest boasts. String many together into a banner to create your own butterfly sanctuary.

rabbit

This little bunny can be reproduced very quickly. Make several. Alternate between having the pattern on the outside or just inside the ears.

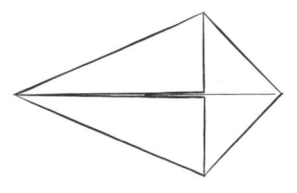

STEP 1: Begin with completed kite base.

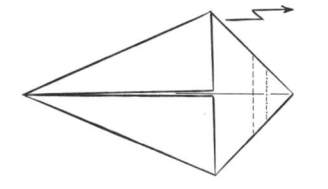

STEP 2: Make a pleat fold.

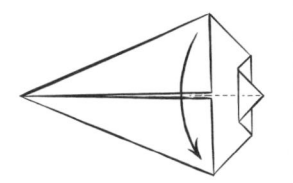

STEP 3: Fold in half horizontally.

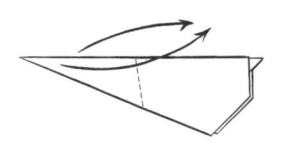

STEP 4: Fold up to make an outside reverse fold.

STEP 5: Cut along crease about two-thirds of the way down. Open up ears to shape them.

completed rabbit

STEP 1: Begin with completed fish base.

STEP 2: Fold top point down.

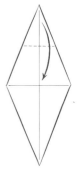

STEP 3: Fold tip down.

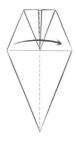

STEP 4: Fold in half horizontally.

STEP 5: Rotate.

STEP 6: Fold tail up to make an inside reverse fold.

STEP 7: Fold fins forward.

completed carp

carp

The carp, called "koi" in Japan, is a classic Japanese icon and is often depicted on colorful kites.

turtle

Turtles are reptiles. They may live on land, or in fresh or salt water. Turtles are slow and steady and can live to a ripe old age.

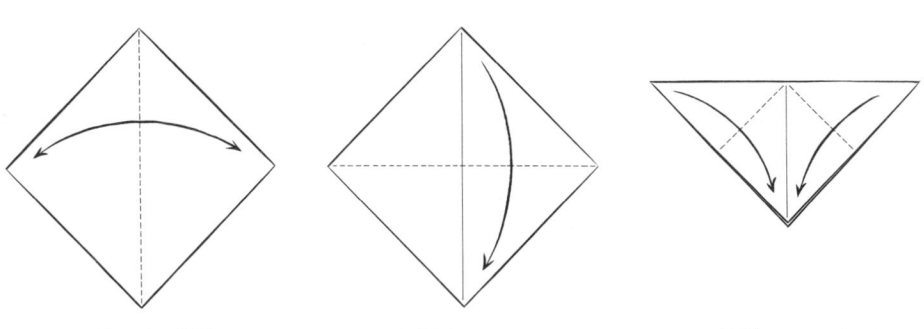

STEP 1: Fold and unfold to create a crease.

STEP 2: Fold down.

STEP 3: Fold corners down.

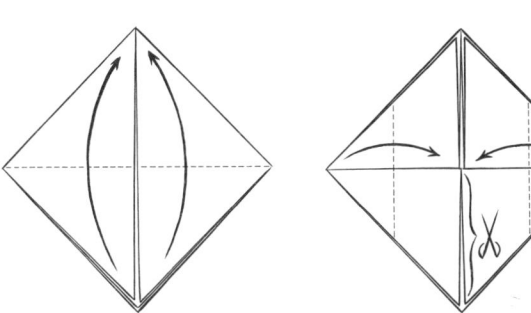
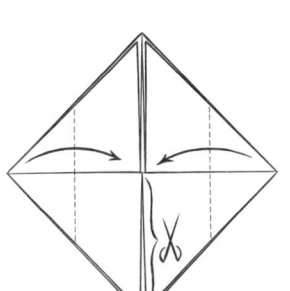

STEP 4: Fold points up.

STEP 5: Cut only the top layer from the bottom point to the center, and fold outside corners in.

STEP 6: Fold points out.

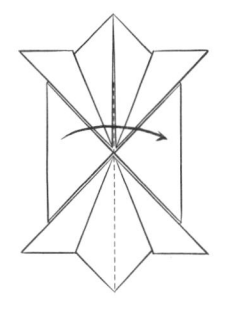
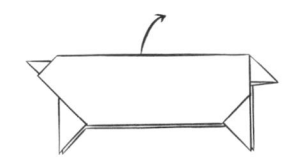

STEP 7: Fold in half horizontally.

STEP 8: Make a straight pleat fold for the tail, and an angled pleat fold for the head.

STEP 9: Unfold.

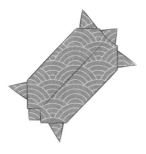

completed turtle

dove

A dove can symbolize both peace and love. What the world needs now is more doves!

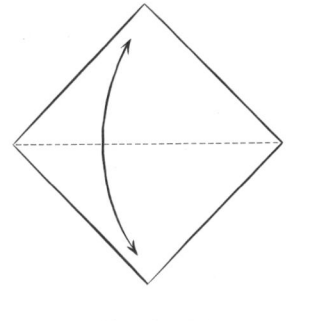

STEP 1: Fold and unfold to create a crease.

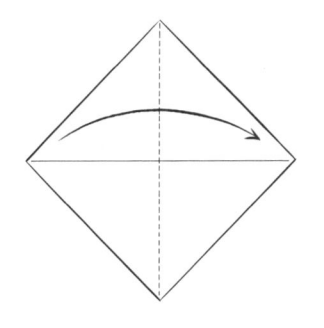

STEP 2: Fold in half.

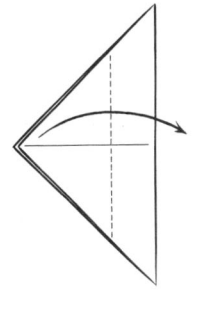

STEP 3: Fold over about two-thirds.

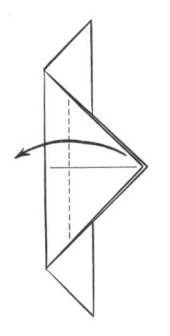

STEP 4: Fold only the top layer over about three-quarters.

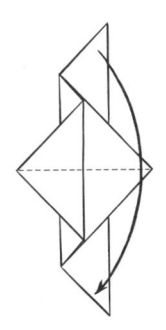

STEP 5: Fold down.

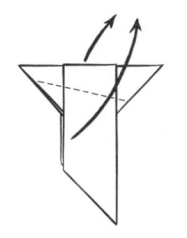

STEP 6: Fold the wings up.

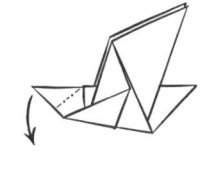

STEP 7: Make an inside reverse fold for the dove's head.

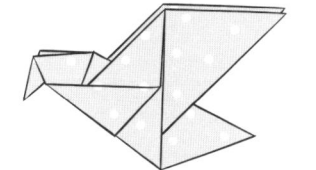

completed dove

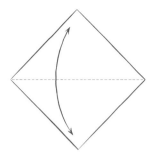

STEP 1: Fold and unfold to create a crease.

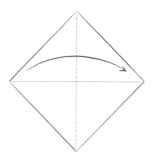

STEP 2: Fold in half.

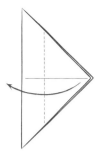

STEP 3: Fold over about two-thirds.

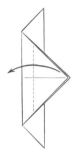

STEP 4: Fold only the top layer over about three-quarters.

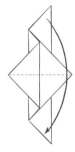

STEP 5: Fold down.

STEP 6: Fold the wings up.

STEP 7: Fold down.

STEP 8: Make an inside reverse fold for the tail.

STEP 9: (Head detail) Make a pleat fold and an inside reverse fold for the eagle's beak.

eagle

Eagles are birds of prey noted for their keen vision and powers of flight. Occasionally, these origami eagles have been known to fly, too.

completed eagle

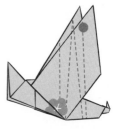

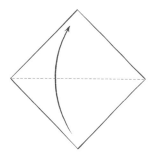

STEP 1: Fold up.

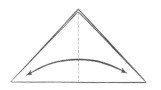

STEP 2: Fold and unfold.

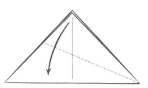

STEP 3: Fold top layer down.

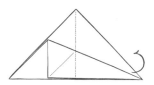

STEP 4: Fold right corner behind.

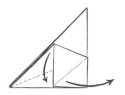

STEP 5: Fold out while folding down.

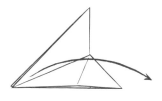

STEP 6: Fold upper layer over.

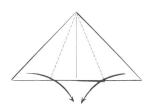

STEP 7: Fold outer corners in toward center.

STEP 8: Fold in half.

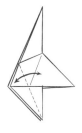

STEP 9: Fold and unfold. (Repeat on backside.)

goose

Geese mate for life, so do this pretty goose a favor and fold up a gander, too.

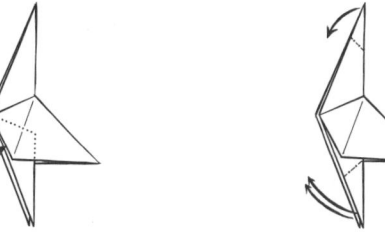

STEP 10: *Tuck under flap. (Repeat on backside.)*

STEP 11: *Make inside reverse folds for head and feet.*

completed goose

STEP 1: Begin with a completed kite base.

STEP 2: Turn over.

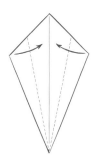

STEP 3: Fold outer corners in toward center.

STEP 4: Turn over.

STEP 5: Fold in half.

STEP 6: Rotate.

STEP 7: Make an outside reverse fold for the neck.

STEP 8: Make another outside reverse fold for the head.

♂wan

Like geese, swans mate for life. Because of their beauty, swans are an enduring symbol of love and fidelity.

completed swan

STEP 1: Begin with a completed diamond base.

STEP 2: Fold in half.

STEP 3: Rotate.

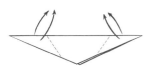

STEP 4: Make outside reverse folds for the neck and tail. (The neck should be a bit taller than the tail.)

STEP 5: Make an outside reverse fold for the head, and an inside reverse fold for the tail.

STEP 6: Fold the bottom corners under.

STEP 7: Make a pleat fold for the duck's bill.

completed duck

duck

Sticky-backed magnet tape is readily available in craft supply stores. Small squares of this tape affixed to a family of ducklings make for adorable refrigerator magnets.

cicada

The cicada is known for his distinctive song. Only the male cicada sings, often to find a mate.

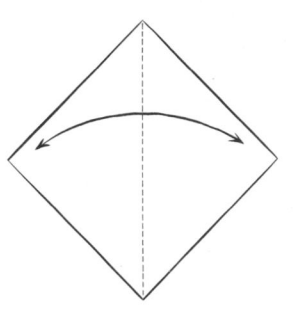

STEP 1: Fold and unfold to create a crease.

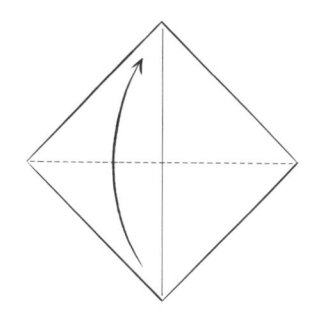

STEP 2: Fold up.

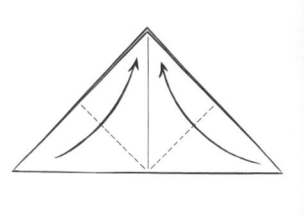

STEP 3: Fold corners up.

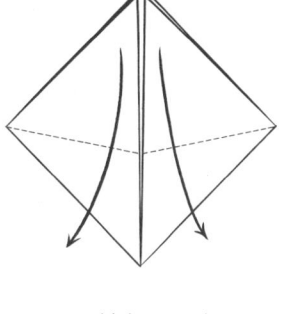

STEP 4: Fold down and slightly out.

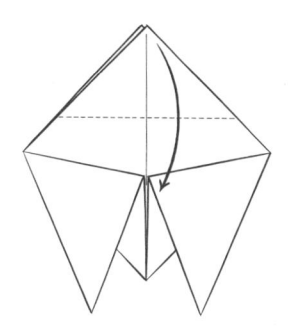

STEP 5: Fold only the uppermost layer down.

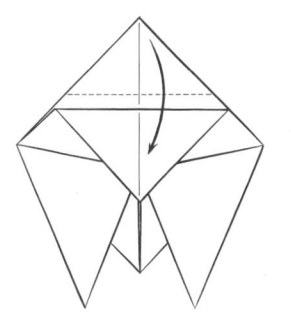

STEP 6: Fold the back layer down a bit farther up from upper-layer fold.

STEP 7: Turn over.

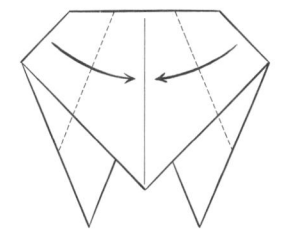

STEP 8: Fold the sides in toward the center.

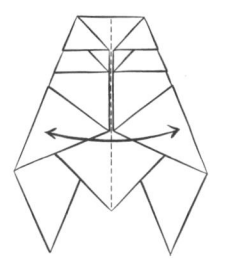

STEP 9: Fold and unfold.

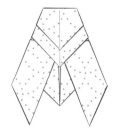

STEP 10: Turn over.

completed cicada

penguin

With its adorable waddle and its curious look, a penguin is a very appealing bird. This little waddler is very simple to make.

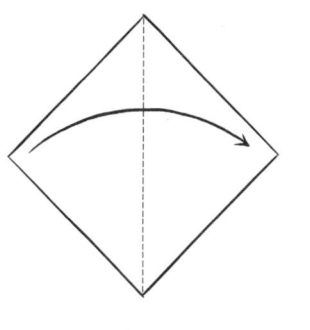

STEP 1: Fold in half.

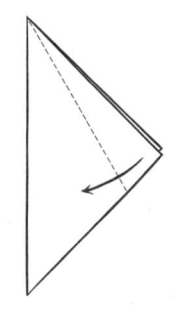

STEP 2: Fold outer corner in and repeat on the backside.

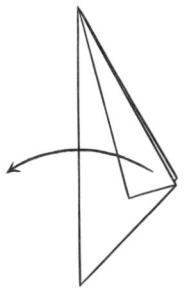

STEP 3: Unfold.

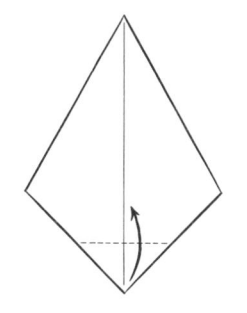

STEP 4: Fold up.

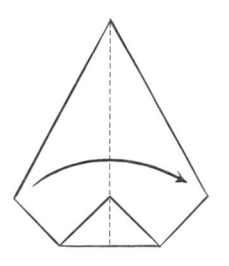

STEP 5: Fold in half.

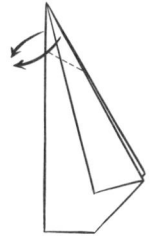

STEP 6: Make an outside reverse fold for the head.

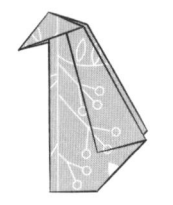

completed penguin

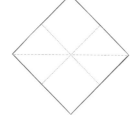

STEP 1: Cut a piece of paper into quarters.

STEP 2: Make four preliminary bases, but omit the valley fold between the top and bottom corners. (Set two of the preliminary bases aside for what will become the bodies of the pair of fish. The remaining two will be made into tails.)

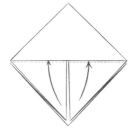

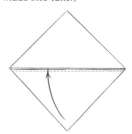

STEP 3: Fold and unfold the uppermost layer of one of the preliminary bases, then tuck it up inside of the base.

STEP 4: Fold and unfold the next layer, and tuck it up inside as well.

STEP 5: Tuck the bottom layer up inside. (Repeat steps 3 through 5 to make the second tail.)

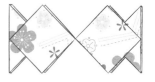

STEP 6: Insert the tabs in the middle of the body into the slits in the front of the tail.

(Repeat for the second fish.)

completed pair of kissing fish

kissing fish

Goldfish are relatively little, and they enjoy having company. Use smaller pieces of paper to make a pair of friendly fish.

peacock

As is typical in the critter kingdom, it is the male of the species who is blessed with extravagant plumage. This project uses colorful paper to great advantage, the folds resulting in a beautiful fan.

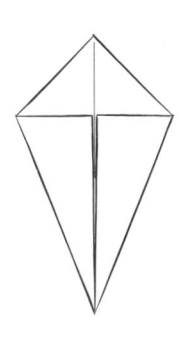

STEP 1: Begin with a completed kite base.

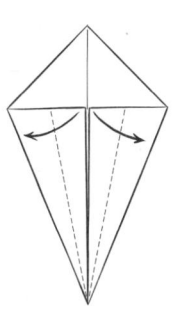

STEP 2: Fold corners out.

STEP 3: Turn over.

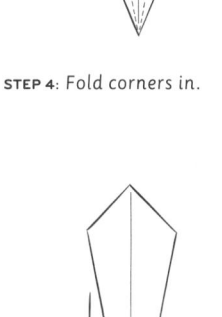

STEP 4: Fold corners in.

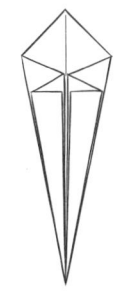

STEP 5: Turn over.

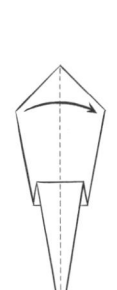

STEP 6: Make a pleat fold.

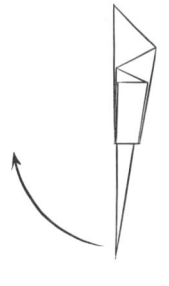

STEP 7: Fold in half, lengthwise.

STEP 8: Fold up.

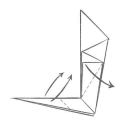  

STEP 9: Make an outside reverse fold for the neck, and fold the outer layer of the tail out. (Repeat on backside.)

STEP 10: Make another outside reverse fold for the head, and fold the next layer of the tail out. (Repeat on backside.)

STEP 11: Pull the outer corners down to fan out the tail.

completed peacock

crane

The crane is the most celebrated of origami shapes. An ancient Japanese legend promises that anyone who folds a thousand paper cranes will be granted a wish.

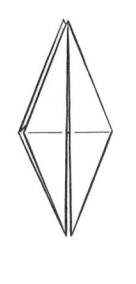

STEP 1: Begin with a completed bird base.

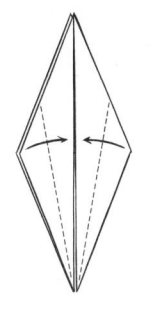

STEP 2: Fold the corners of the upper layer in toward the center. (Repeat on backside.)

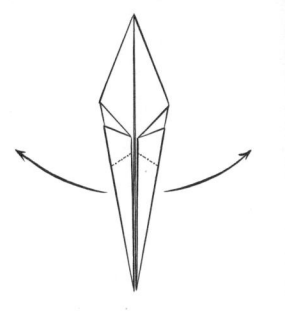

STEP 3: Make an inside reverse fold on both sides for the neck and tail.

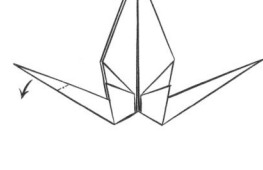

STEP 4: Make an inside reverse fold for the head.

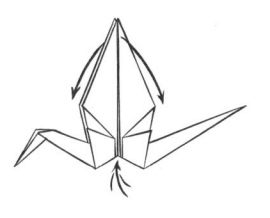

STEP 5: Pull the wings down, and inflate the body a bit by blowing into the center.

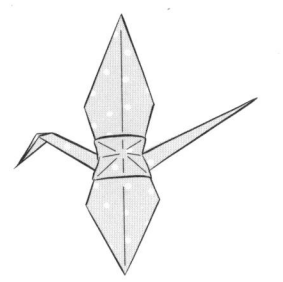

completed crane

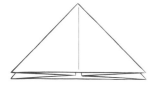

STEP 1: Begin with a completed triangle base.

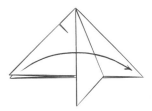

STEP 2: Cut a slit through the two layers on the left, and then fold the uppermost corner on the right side down.

STEP 3: Fold the uppermost layer on the left side over.

STEP 4: Turn over.

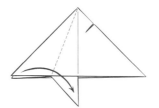

STEP 5: Fold the uppermost layer on the left side down.

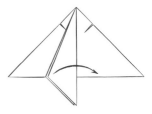

STEP 6: Fold the uppermost layer on the left side over.

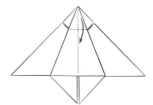

STEP 7: Fold the top down.

STEP 8: Fold the outer corners in.

completed bat

bat

Whether you are a true bat lover or perhaps not so fond of these curious little mammals, there is no denying that this paper version is pretty cute.

dragonfly

Did you know that dragonflies are the world's fastest insects? In Japan, the dragonfly is a symbol of strength and courage.

STEP 1: Begin with a completed bird base.

STEP 2: Fold the uppermost layer on the right side over.

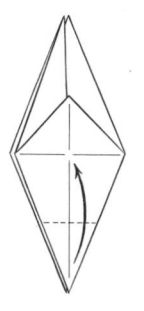

STEP 3: Fold the uppermost layer on the bottom up.

STEP 4: Fold the uppermost layer on the left over.

STEP 5: Fold the uppermost corners on the sides in toward the center. (Repeat on backside.)

STEP 6: Fold and unfold the front wing down. (Repeat on backside.)

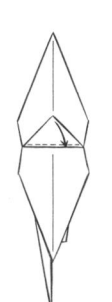

STEP 7: Tuck the triangle in between the wings.

STEP 8: Turn over.

STEP 9: Make an outside reverse fold on both sides for the head and tail.

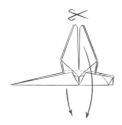

STEP 9: Cut a slit down the center of the wings, and shape the tips with scissors. Fold the wings down.

completed dragonfly

dragonfly

hamster

This little critter really has some dimension to him. After folding him up, fatten him up with a puff of air.

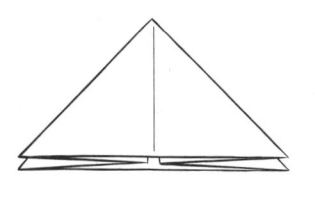

STEP 1: Begin with a completed triangle base.

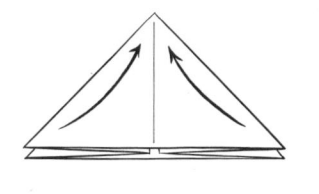

STEP 2: Fold the uppermost corners on the outside up.

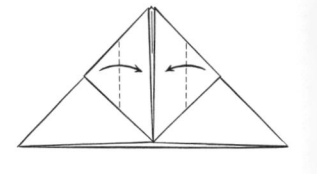

STEP 3: Fold the uppermost corners on the outside in.

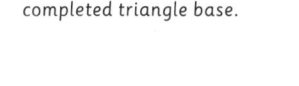

STEP 4: Fold the top corners down.

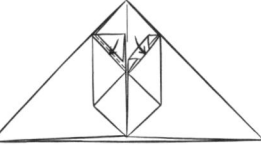

STEP 5: Tuck the corners into the slits.

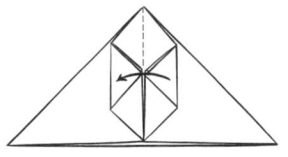

STEP 6: Fold the uppermost layer on the right side over.

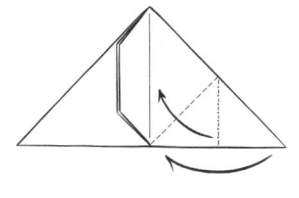

STEP 7: Fold the triangle on the right in half diagonally so that the bottom edge meets the center, and fold the tip of the triangle toward the bottom.

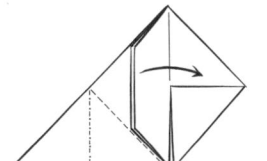

STEP 8: Fold the two uppermost layers on the left over, then repeat the previous step with the triangle on the left.

STEP 9: Turn over.

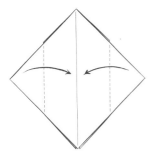

STEP 10: Fold the outside corners in.

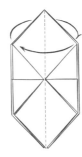

STEP 11: Fold the uppermost layer on the right over to the left, then fold the back layer on the left behind to the right.

STEP 12: Rotate.

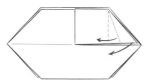

STEP 13: Push in to make a squash fold for the ear by folding the uppermost layer over, then pulling the top of that layer back, and folding down into a diamond. (Repeat on backside.)

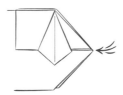

STEP 14: Pinch the top together while blowing into the hole in the front of the hamster to inflate.

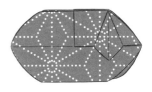

completed hamster

angelfish

These beauties are common in aquariums and are easily recognized by their long, flowing fins. Fold up a family and hang them from string to create a colorful aquarium mobile.

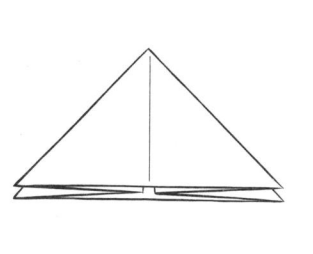

STEP 1: Begin with a completed triangle base.

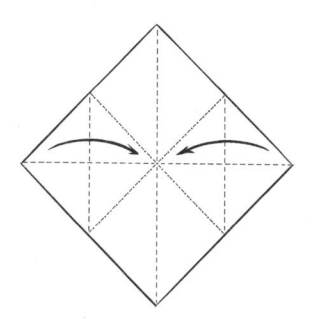

STEP 2: Unfold the triangle base, and fold the outside corners in toward the center.

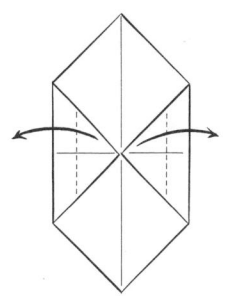

STEP 3: Fold the inside corners out.

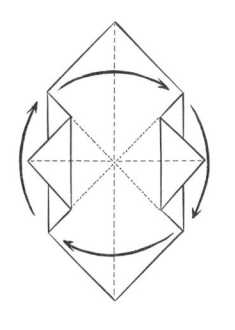

STEP 4: Refold back into the triangle base.

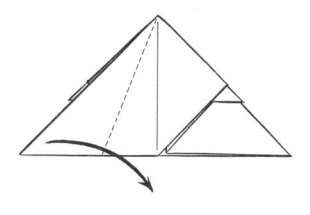

STEP 5: Fold the left corner down. (Repeat on backside.)

STEP 6: Rotate.

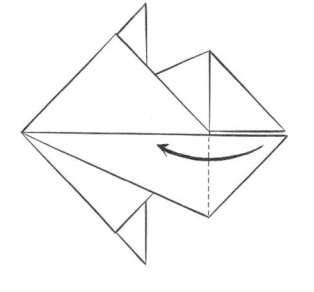

STEP 7: Fold the tail in. (Repeat on backside.)

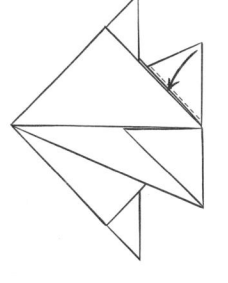

STEP 8: Tuck the top part of the tail inside the body, then repeat with the bottom part of the tail.

completed angelfish

STEP 1: Begin with a completed bird base.

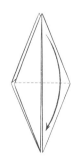

STEP 2: Fold the top down.

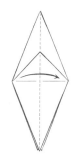

STEP 3: Fold in half.

STEP 4: Rotate.

STEP 5: Make an inside reverse fold for the upper segment of the leg. (Repeat on backside.)

STEP 6: Make another inside reverse fold for the lower segment of the leg. (Repeat on backside.)

STEP 7: Make an outside reverse fold for the head.

STEP 8: Head detail. Make a slit in the crease for the antennae, and fold them forward.

completed grasshopper

grasshopper

Walk, hop, or fly, the grasshopper can do it all.

honey bee

Bees do much more than pollinate flowers and make honey. They are unsung heroes of agriculture. Where would we be without bees?

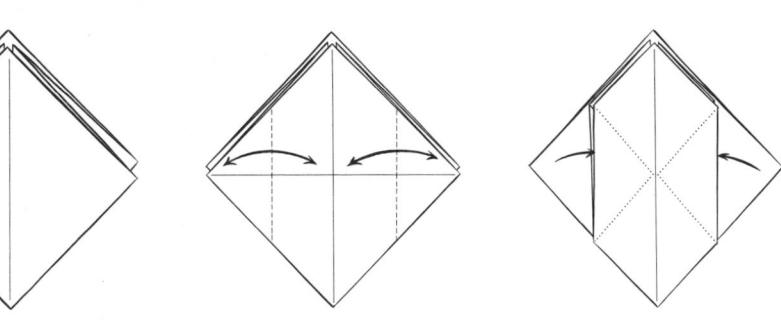

STEP 1: Begin with a completed upside down preliminary base.

STEP 2: Fold and unfold the outside corners of the uppermost layer.

STEP 3: Tuck the corners inside with an inside reverse fold. (Repeat on backside.)

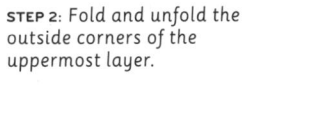

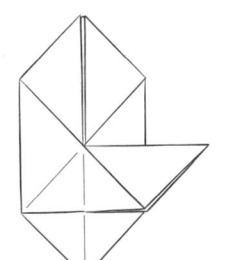

STEP 4: Fold and unfold the uppermost layer diagonally to the left and right. (Repeat on backside.)

STEP 5: Bring the sides in together and fold down to the right. (Repeat on backside.)

STEP 6: Fold the top two layers on the right over to the left. (Repeat on backside.)

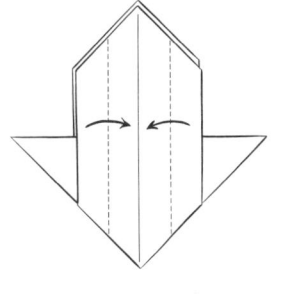

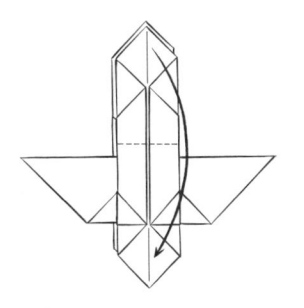

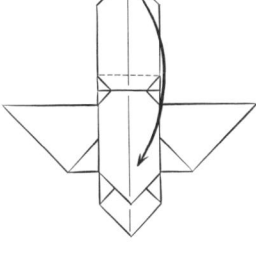

STEP 7: Fold the uppermost layers in. (Repeat on backside.)

STEP 8: Fold the uppermost layer down just above the top of the wings.

STEP 9: Fold the back layer down just above the previous one.

STEP 10: Fold the wings in.

completed honey
bee

honey bee

seal

A few small snips make the seal's cute and characteristic whiskers in this picture-perfect project.

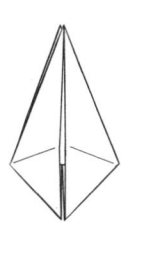

STEP 1: Begin with a completed fish base.

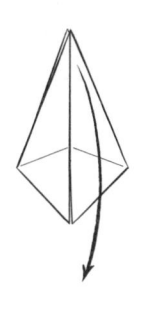

STEP 2: Fold down.

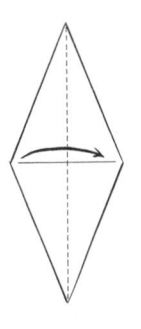

STEP 3: Fold in half.

STEP 4: Rotate.

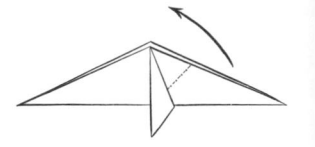

STEP 5: Fold the front flipper forward. (Repeat on backside.)

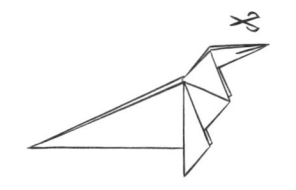

STEP 6: Make an inside reverse fold for the neck.

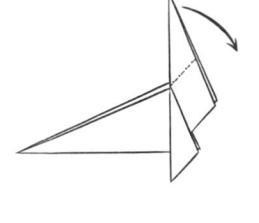

STEP 7: Make another inside reverse fold for the head.

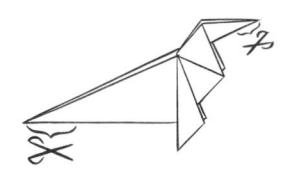

STEP 8: Cut slits in the crease of the face and tail.

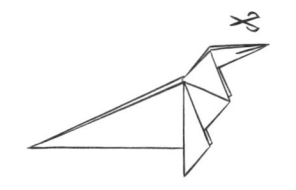

STEP 9: Cut another slit in the center of the face.

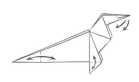

STEP 10: Fold to shape the tail, flippers, and whiskers.

completed seal

seal

chicken

Who isn't a fan of the chicken? This lovely little bird is just looking for a nest.

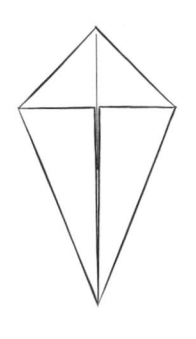

STEP 1: Begin with a completed kite base.

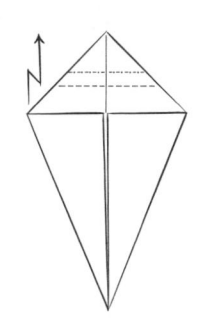

STEP 2: Make a pleat fold.

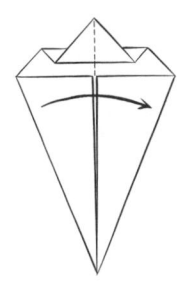

STEP 3: Fold in half.

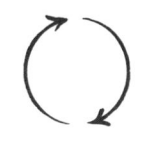

STEP 4: Rotate.

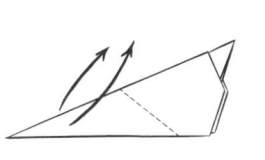

STEP 5: Make an outside reverse fold for the neck.

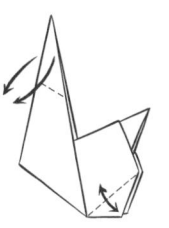

STEP 6: Make another outside reverse fold for the head. Fold and unfold the bottom corner to make the wing tips. (Repeat on backside.)

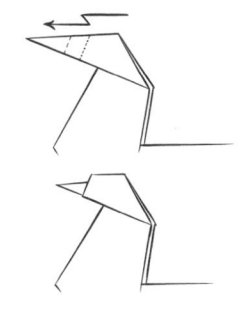

STEP 7: (Head detail.) Make a pleat fold for the beak.

completed chicken

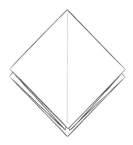

STEP 1: Begin with a completed preliminary base.

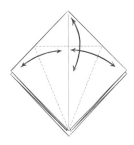

STEP 2: Fold and unfold the outer corners of the uppermost layer, then fold and unfold the top corner down. (Repeat on backside.)

STEP 3: Cut the center of the top and bottom layers up to the crease near the top.

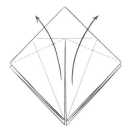

STEP 4: Fold the bottom corners of the uppermost layer up. (Repeat on backside.)

STEP 5: Fold the tips down. (Repeat on backside.)

STEP 6: Fold the outside corners of the uppermost layer in. (Repeat on backside.)

STEP 7: Rotate.

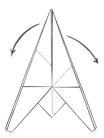

STEP 8: Make an inside reverse fold for both the head and tail.

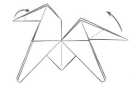

STEP 9: Fold the nose inside, then add a flourish to the tail with another inside reverse fold.

pony

This frisky little high-stepper is lots of fun to make. The spirited tail shows that she is ready for anything.

completed pony

STEP 1: Begin with a completed kite base.

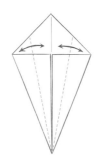

STEP 2: Fold and unfold the outer corners.

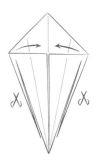

STEP 3: Cut thin strips along the outer folded edges for the antennae, then refold toward the center.

STEP 4: Fold the upper corners in.

STEP 5: Cut a slit about half way between the tip and the point where the folds meet.

STEP 6: Make a pleat fold on either side of the slit.

STEP 7: Pass the antennae strips through the slit, then fold down around the back.

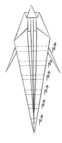

STEP 8: Make about six pleat folds along the body of the shrimp.

STEP 9: Fold in half.

shrimp

A few snips form the long antennae of the shrimp in this project. The antennae are critical to this cute crustacean—how else would he scout out a snack in his sandy environs?

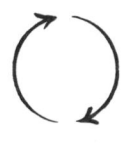

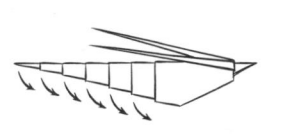

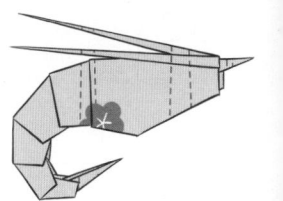

STEP 10: Rotate.

STEP 11: Pull each of the pleats down to curve the body.

completed shrimp